P R E F A

Where Have All The Children Gone? is the first of three books that comprise The Trilogy of Growth. It is written through the eyes of a child who questions, "What does it mean to be a grown-up?" The child looks to adults in her world to see what examples each offers. She questions the compromises, the risks, the benefits and realities of choosing to become a grown-up.

These are difficult times for children growing up today. More than ever before, boys and girls are hungry for adult models who are trustworthy, credible and loving. The book is written out of my own memories of childhood and experiences as an educator, international lecturer and mother of two grown children. It is written for grown-ups to playfully reflect on the models they offer the children in their lives.

This book is also written for the child within each of us. Hopefully we never lose touch with that core sense of self. With delightful illustrations the book invites you, the reader, to recommit yourself to wonder, to play and to redefining what and who are most important in your life. It offers insights into how we might *"Grow Deep - Not Just Tall."* It challenges us to remember that *"Life is Change - Growth is Optional."*

Other Books by Karen Kaiser Clark
Published by CEP, Inc.

Grow Deep - Not Just Tall
Life is Change - Growth is Optional

S omeday I'll be one too. A grown -up! I don't know if I want to be one... but I'm afraid I don't have a choice about it. It seems the children part of people just goes away and boys and girls become grown-ups.

I wonder what it means to be a grown-up. Does it mean more than getting big? What does "mature" mean? My grandma says it's what some grown-ups are. She says, "Few of us ever really mature. Most of us just grow up tall." I wonder what she means.

I wonder about a lot of things. Kids do that.

I wonder if God can see the color of my eyes even when I'm sleeping.

I wonder where the white goes when the snow melts.

I wonder what flowers think of people and who wins wars.

I wonder if grown-ups ever wonder.

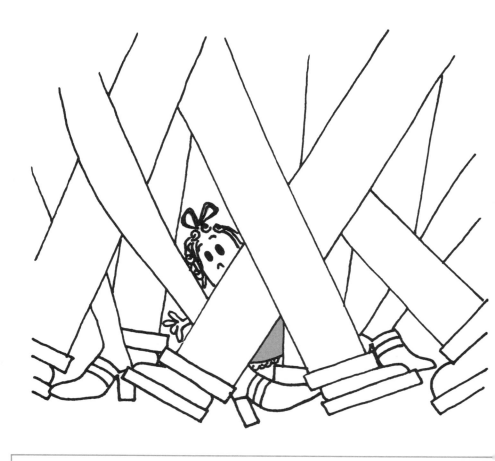

Grown-ups are always in such a hurry. Then they complain about not having time to grow. I wonder why. I wrote a poem about them.

Grown-Ups

There go the grown-ups,

forever rushing, filled with answers,

always in control.

I wish that they would listen just

a little more to me.

I wonder if they question all those

things they seem so sure of.

Standing so much taller,

they have a lot more power.

At times I feel frightened and unseen.

I wonder if the me today will simply disappear,

when I am all grown-up and one of them.

I hope not.

DAILY NE

MAN SEES BIRD

Why do grown-ups do so many things? Often I see them doing at least two things at one time. Like my mom, she doesn't just watch T.V. She knits, reads the paper, watches T. V. and wiggles her foot all at the same time. Not my dad though. He does just one thing at a time. Seldom does he have time to just sit and be with me.

When you're a grown-up you have to plan a lot. You have to get ready for what's going to happen next. You have to wrinkle up your forehead and worry.

It must be sad not being able to just jump up and do whatever pops into your mind or just get all excited.

I like to be silly. I think it's fun to really laugh right out loud. Most grown-ups seem so serious. They are always i n what they call, "control."

It must be hard not to be able to giggle and to always have to keep your voice down. Except, of course, when you're scolding someone. Then all the rules change.

There are so many things you have to do when you're a grown-up. You have to talk on the telephone for hours, make lists of things to do and lists of your lists. Then, when you're over forty, you have to try and find them.

You have to go on all kinds of diets too, and talk about food all the time. Grown-ups have to know how to fix up checkbooks and zippers that won't zip.

They even have to go into dark basements all alone to change fuses.

Grown-ups have a hard time making up their minds.

Saturday, Mom told me to clean my room. She said, "Get in here and get up there and clean that room! Why can't you be like Marion? She is such a good helper. Her mother doesn't have to scold. Plus, Marion uses hangers not doorknobs!"

Marion WAS my best friend. But, right then, I didn't even like her.

However, that all changed back on Sunday, when I asked Mom if I could stay up until 9:30 because Marion got to. My mom looked at me and said, "And who cares what Marion does! You live in this house and our rule is 9:00." Grown-ups really confuse me.

One of the things that most confuses me is why grown-ups don't cry. They don't do it when they fall down hard and get skinned up on the outside. That makes me wonder if they cry when they get hurt on the inside. Like, when your best friend tells you you're only her second best friend. Maybe grown-ups can't cry.

I know they have tears though. I saw one ONCE on my daddy's cheek. He was watching "Bonanza" on television. He didn't know I saw it. I think he was nervous trying to figure out what to do with it.

I wonder what happens to all the tears inside of grown-ups. Does the hurting part just stay inside of them?

It scares me to think of being a grown-up. You have to give up so many things. You have to be so careful of what you say and what you do and of what other people think of you.

When I'm a grown-up I guess I won't be able to come right out and ask somebody to hold me when I'm afraid or when I'm sad. Grown-ups are supposed to be strong. Aren't they?

I won't be able to wrestle in *my* daddy's arms and whisper secrets like, "I love you, Daddy." I'll have to learn how to stand tall and shake hands.

I won't be able to scratch wherever I itch or have contests to see who can burp the loudest.

Maybe being grown-up means hiding a lot of my inside feelings and thoughts.

How do you do that? Who will teach me? Will I learn these things in school?

Some of the things about being a grown-up scare me but not everything. Big people have a lot of neat things too. They can say things that kids get spanked for saying. They get to stay up late and decide what to eat. Plus, grown-ups have the last word on just about everything. Sometimes they don't even have to say, "I'm sorry."

I like to play games and to pretend. I wonder if grown-ups do. Once my mom told me about a kind of big people's halloween party. She called it a class reunion. She said when it came time to take off the masks, no one did. I wonder how anyone knew who anyone else really was. Grown-ups do pretend, don't they!

I don't understand a lot about being big. But big people don't understand how hard it is to be little. They keep looking down at me and saying, "These are the best years of your life."

Oh, if they only knew all the problems I have. For example, this morning Kevin spilled orange paint on my new sweater and my mother doesn't know yet. Then I got blamed for two things I didn't do. . . this time. . . and no one would even listen to my side of the story. Tomorrow is Kelli's birthday party and I'm not even invited yet. Boy, if I ever am a grown-up and have kids, I'm going to remember what it's like to be little.

Well, when the day comes when I absolutely have to be a grown-up maybe I can be the neat kind. That's the shrinking kind of grown-up like my grandmas and grandpas. The older they get the shorter they get instead of growing taller.

They are really special people. They don't always understand kids but they love them a lot anyway. They're just great! They go for "slow" walks and pop popcorn even when it's not a weekend. Grandparents have time.

They grow beautiful flowers in gardens and inside their houses by sunny windows. They sometimes scold but almost never give spankings.

Grandpas don't tell you what you're supposed to do. They just like you the way you are. Grandpas can tell stories like nobody else can and they always have quarters and candies in their pockets. They tease too in a fun way that doesn't hurt and most important, they really listen to me.

My grandpa even likes to hear me practice on the piano. He says, "It's beautiful," and he means it.

Grandmas let you have treats between meals. They use hankies not tissues. Grandmas have soft laps for cuddling and bumpy fingers. When grandmas sing in church it sounds like warbling.

Grandmas save everything; little surprises I make for them and pictures that I draw. They even save presents they get for their birthdays. I know because once I peeked in my grandma's dresser drawer and saw three pretty slips we had given her, all tucked away in white tissue paper.

Grandparents know how to pretend and how to just be with you. They understand how little things can be very important. They even know how to cry.

My grandma cries when she hears something sad on the news. I see my grandpa cry whenever he reads a letter from my oldest cousin in college. He says it's because he is so proud of her. Grandmas and Grandpas really know how to care and to love.

But grandparents are old. Maybe it's even hard being a wrinkled-up grown-up. They have to take naps again just like children. They have to be careful not to run fast or to lift heavy things. Their knees hurt, and their teeth come out at night.

Sometimes they have to go to the doctors and take great-big pills. Grandmas wear such funny looking underwear. My grandpa has to wear a locket with little white pills in it for his heart.

I guess it's not easy even when you're an old grown-up. Besides, my grandpa says it's sometimes kind of lonely.

Someday I'll be one too. A grown-up. I guess I don't have a choice about that. I'm afraid it's never going to be easy but I do think I can decide what kind of grown-up I'll be.

When it happens to me I hope I'll be some of the today me. When I'm big I hope I'll still remember what it's like to be little. I hope I'll grow deep and not just tall. Maybe I'll be that word my grandma says, "mature."

I hope I'll be like my mom and dad and a lot like my grandmas and my grandpas. Most of all, I hope I'll honestly and fully be who I am meant to be and that is . . . ME!

"The End"

WHERE HAVE ALL THE CHILDREN GONE?
GONE TO GROWN-UPS, EVERYONE!

As we become "grown-ups" we may lose touch with the spirit of the child deep inside of us. If that happens, life may seem little more than one problem after another. As we accept adult responsibilities some of us forget how to play, how to celebrate moments, how to risk being honest about our feelings. For many a crisis or another birthday may prompt them to realize that something is missing. Some say that becoming grandparents sparks that sense of joy, hope and honesty they once knew . . . so long ago.

Learning to rekindle the spirit of the child within us can begin now! Based on her first book, **Where Have All The Children Gone?** this keynote session examines the six characteristics of persons who awaken the child within and who risk to **Grow Deep—Not Just Tall**.

I. SENSE OF WONDER
Aristotle said that "wonder is the first cause of philosophy." If we cease to wonder we limit our vision. Life may then become a matter of parochial absolutes. Choose to question, to marvel, to imagine, to wonder. Awaken the mind of the child within you.

II. EXCITEMENT FOR LIVING
A sense of enthusiasm, joy and hope are critical components of quality living. Learning to prioritize, to set boundaries and to nurture one's self can elevate a sense of excitement for the gift of another day. Nurture your sense of humor.

III. FREEDOM TO CHOOSE
It is not what happens to us that makes or breaks us. Rather, it is how we choose to perceive and to respond to our circumstances. Those decisions mark the differences between our becoming victims, survivors or courageous victors in life.

IV. EMBRACING VULNERABILITY
At times we "let a grown-up pride hide all the need inside and act more like children than children." Acknowledging vulnerability is essential if we choose to develop a genuine sense of self, admirable integrity and real strength.

V. MEANING-FULL CONNECTIONS
Life is not meant to be lived in isolation. It is a journey meant to be shared. Invest in meaning-full, honest and healthy relationships. That requires respect-full acknowledgement of individuals' uniqueness, similarities and diversity.

VI. MYSTERY IN LIFE
Life is more than we can intellectually comprehend or emotionally experience. The possibilities offered by technology can never exceed the awesome potentials awaiting those who live life with their hearts and souls as well as their heads.

This outline is just one of many keynote presentations by Karen Kaiser Clark. She lectures internationally on the concepts included in her three books.
For more information contact

CEP PUBLICATIONS 13119 Heritage Way, Suite 1200
St. Paul, Minnesota 55124 (952) 454-1163

CEP PUBLICATIONS BOOKS

A TRILOGY OF GROWTH

Written by Karen Kaiser Clark, these three books are intertwined. From differing perspectives and in a natural progression, each book invites the reader to discover how growth can flourish if one chooses to change.

Where Have All The Children Gone?
Gone to Grown-Ups ,Everyone!

Delightfully illustrated and appealing to all ages, this book looks at the adult world through the eyes of a child. It challenges us to see maturity not as a goal to be achieved but as a continuous process of growth to be experienced. It invites the reader to rediscover the child within.

Grow Deep Not Just Tall

A wise and weathered oak tree teaches us how to grow through each of the seasons of our lives. It challenges us to change and grow.

Life is Change — Growth is Optional

Having survived cruel storms that threatened to destroy her, the oak tree "grows deeper" in the face of misfortune. She learns how to ask for help, to reroot, to reach out and to risk to embrace life once again. Powerfully illustrated, this book is a source of hope and comfort for those striving to grow through the unfair seasons of their lives.

TAPES
Audio Cassette Tapes
Featuring Karen Kaiser Clark

Where Have All The Children Gone?
A reading of the book and a 60 minute development of the characteristics of ever-increasing maturity.

Grow Deep, Not Just Tall
A 90 minute reading of the book accompanied with music.

Life is Change — Growth is Optional
A 60 minute presentation on the symbolic meanings of the seasons of our lives.

For information on Karen Kaiser Clark as a keynote speaker or consultant for your organization or convention, contact CEP, 13119 Heritage Way, St. Paul, Minnesota 55124. Telephone: 952/454-1163.

GROW DEEP - NOT JUST TALL

Rekindling a sense of hope and joy in our lives
Based on her book *Where Have All The Children Gone*
Presented by Karen Kaiser Clark

As we become "grown-ups" we may lose touch with the spirit of the child deep inside of us. Life begins to feel little more than one problem after another. In time a sense of weariness or another birthday may prompt us to realize that something is missing. Many say that becoming grandparents sparks a sense of joy and hope they once celebrated long ago.

Living responsibly with genuine enthusiasm, hope and joy can begin today. Rekindling a zest for life is the cornerstone of "growing deep - not just tall." It is what we must rediscover if we want to really live our lives fully and not merely survive.

Using multimedia, group participation and a healthy dose of humor this session invites you to explore:

* The six characteristics of genuine maturity
  1) **Capacity for Wonder**   4) **Acknowledging vulnerability**
  2) **Enthusiasm for Life**   5) **Meaning-full Relationships**
  3) **Personal Responsibility** 6) **A Sense of Mystery**

* Nurturing a sense of hope and joy
  1) **Playfulness vs. Competition**
  2) **Believing is Seeing vs. Seeing is Believing**

* Four steps to unlearn old attitudes and habits

* The magic of risking imperfection

* Practicing the skills of listening with the heart
  1) **Focusing**   2) **Acceptance**   3) **Clarifying**

* Rediscovering the miraculous in the common

©Karen Kaiser Clark - 13119 Heritage Way-Suite 1200
St. Paul, MN 55124 - 952/454-1163

LIFE IS CHANGE
GROWTH IS OPTIONAL

The power of personal choice in facing life's challenges
Based on her book *Life is Change - Growth is Optional*
Presented by Karen Kaiser Clark

The only constant in life is change. We must learn to prepare for change, to positively initiate it in our lives and to cope with its consequences. No culture has ever been more challenged by such explosive technology, elevated insecurity and phenomenal opportunities for growth. How we respond is an individual choice each must make and a responsibility each must own.

Paralleling the four seasons of life this session examines the personal and professional process of change. Using multimedia, group participation and a healthy dose of humor this session will focus on the specifics of:

* The four seasons and the cycles of change
   "The whole of life is greater that the sum of its separated seasons."

 * The power of perception in facing reality
   "Believing is seeing - Reclaiming realistic expectations"

 * Releasing old routines, bad habits, rigid vision
   "The difference between a rut and a grave is the depth of the hole."

* The four essential characteristics of Believers in Life
   "Choice - Challenge - Connections - Courage"

* The process of growth in taking care of one's self
   "One can only give what he/she has to offer."

 * The price of changing and consequences of not
   "Destiny may shape our ends but we can shape our middles."

©Karen Kaiser Clark - 13119 Heritage Way*Suite 1200
St. Paul, MN 55124 - 952/454-1163

CEP PUBLICATIONS BOOKS

THE CENTER FOR EXECUTIVE PLANNING, INC.

13119 Heritage Way, Suite 1200 • St. Paul, Minnesota, 55124
Telephone: 952/454-1163

Name: _____

Street Address: _____

City: _____ State: _____ Zip: _____

O R D E R   F O R M

B O O K S

WHERE HAVE ALL THE CHILDREN GONE?

COPIES _____   COST PER BOOK $ 9.95   TOTAL $ _____

GROW DEEP, NOT JUST TALL

COPIES _____   COST PER BOOK $ 12.95   TOTAL $ _____

LIFE IS CHANGE — GROWTH IS OPTIONAL

COPIES _____   COST PER BOOK $ 16.95   TOTAL $ _____

T A P E S

WHERE HAVE ALL THE CHILDREN GONE?

COPIES _____   COST PER TAPE $ 9.95   TOTAL $ _____

GROW DEEP, NOT JUST TALL

COPIES _____   COST PER TAPE $ 9.95   TOTAL $ _____

LIFE IS CHANGE — GROWTH IS OPTIONAL

COPIES _____   COST PER TAPE $ 9.95   TOTAL $ _____

SUBTOTAL $ _____

SHIPPING & HANDLING	
ORDERS TO $15.00..........ADD	$3.00
15.00 TO $25.00.......ADD	$3.50
25.00 TO $50.00.......ADD	$4.00
50.00 AND OVER ....ADD	$5.50

MINNESOTA RESIDENTS ADD 6.5% SALES TAX **TAX** $ _____

SHIPPING & HANDLING TOTAL $ _____

ENCLOSED IS MY CHECK OR MONEY ORDER TO CEP: **TOTAL** $ _____